Come down Cunderang
by John Millett

POETRY Australia

Number 99, 1985

Editor: Grace Perry

Published by SOUTH HEAD PRESS

*with the assistance of the Literature Board of the
Australia Council, the N.S.W. Government
Advisory Committee on Cultural Grants, and
The Peter Stuyvesant Cultural Foundation.*

JAMES ROWAN CALLAGHAN died in 1984. A specific bequest in his will provided for the collation and publication of his writings and other documents relating to six generations of the Callaghans of Cunderang.

This book is an abstract of material hoarded in a big box on which he had written:

> In any age
> genes are wild cards
> about to be tossed
> diverse
> autonomous
> held loosely together.

First published in 1985 by
SOUTH HEAD PRESS
The Market Place, Berrima, NSW 2577
© South Head Press 1985
National Library of Australia
card number and ISBN 0 909 185 20 4
Wholly set up and printed in Australia by Hogbin, Poole (Printers) Pty. Ltd.
99 Marriott Street, Redfern, NSW 2016

BOOK 1

GREEN JACKET REELS AND A JIG

Whether you take the crest of Mount Werrikimber
as a mark
or the line of a snake's belly
as a level
let their day present itself

A lady horse with a golden stride
called to the King of the Stallions
(him with jewels in his semen
white as ferns in the frost)

an appletree laughed
and gurt diddicky
that old appleman
fathered a whole orchard with one seed.

Great laughter in bronze

Cunderang in the Parish of Werriker County of Vernon State of New South Wales is a place like the harp of old Ireland that has the sweetest notes and most prolonged sleeping in the hills between Seaview and Mount Werrikimber the way a melody waits in the strings.

There is a string of iron called the Soontree, a string of noble bronze, the Gauntree and a string entirely of silver, the Goltree.

Play the merry Gauntree and the hosts of the earth will be laughing. Play the pure Goltree and all will be crying.

Within the Green Islands only those able to hear the wind on a ribbed beach crying in the dry tight sinews of a whale skeleton or beyond the Green Islands those for whom that same wind strokes fibres stretched across the frame of a great horse or any other dead creature so that it makes the deep murmuring of the Soontree, full of sleep – surely they are the ones with the power to know the language of beasts, idiom of water and dust, dialect of trees and even understand the distant chatter of grass on the Plains of Pleasure below Werrikimber – and whether they are on Aran or Madagascar they will surely hear the deep bronze notes of the Gauntree laugh when those same dead fibres come alive against the fingernails of a great harper.

The cowboy of Cunderang dump

This is crow country
stray cat land
vixen and rabbit ground
where young Eamon Callaghan
walks with a Cheyenne roll
death on his hip
authority signed by the Town Clerk
to force the dump to drop its guns

He's rigged to break a hobble strap
in shirt of claypan brown
Cuban heels
crutch itchy from tight bone drill riders
buckled with tooled calf leather silver studded
battered stetson set to the angle of infinity
     He'd screw a concho
     into the daughter of any man
     then throw a longhorn saddle on a buck

     lean trouble shooter
     lips thin as gods
     straddling a flat cutter saddle
     with bell stirrups
     girth cinched
     riding in to clean a junk yard up
     born to fix a death grip on this sod

In April the single willow
takes off its shirt and dies three times
Then he lays baits for wild cats
Rats twitch
and the vixen fires green water at the frost

The land Valhalla

At the perceiving distance
Marcus Callaghan
eternally detached
                        crossed the Barrington
                        heavy with snow
                        up Hungry Hill
                        above Coopracurrupa
                                Swamp Creek
                        near Hell Gate
                        to Cunderang – 1841

and by survey laid out a village
to stop pre-emption
                        2 stores
                        National School
                        Church
                        an Mr Eliot
                        British admiral's son
                        mixing damper
                        flour to the elbows

Patrick Callaghan
                        took slabs of bastard box
                        up Nundle Spur – 1862

Mr. Carlyle Callaghan
                        with a Londonman's long purse
                        chose New Connaught

Robert
            a rough estate on Mount Werriker – 1865

The Australian Agricultural Company
            the residue

            All north of Tillebuster
            sizeable scopes of country for sheep
            took Carlyle's Swamp as well as Albington's
            and Stony Batter

This from the Memory Notes
of Miss Eenie Callaghan
maps of squattage
boundaries limited by moderation
pressures of disagreements
mounted constables
border police
bough yards
bark humpies

Much later by survey pegs
                law suits
                title deeds

        The geological formations
        calcified whitstone
        rotten slate
        intrusive rock
        that hardens
        and alters the contact wall
        from Mullierindi to the Yarrows
        silurian slate to Myrtle Scrub
        basalt on the upper laminae of gorges
        slate below
        blue whitstone
        as on Inishmore

where Oxley perceived in the valley beneath
        "considerable and rapid streams
        entering the finest country
        (or rather park) imaginable"
        The Great North Road
        and the occasional exaggeration
        in the Journals (7/9/1818)

Down the unravelled dark
camp fires greened the cold air
Events soon to be fastened on a race
described as
                "small
                with attenuated limbs
                scarcely able
                to support their bodies
                disgustingly filthy
                approaching deformity"

The events of a journey
reach out long after
new land
called the earth wonder
and they had hungers
taught in dirty books
to pre-empt
for the sake of possession
with a set of prejudices
branded on them

Kings princes people

in that order of profit-taking
leaving the tribe which lived there

nothing

The land Valhalla
above the caps of snow
and deeds of men
the spinel stars

The three brothers – Aran 1845

Old Michael the fisherman half-blind, father of nine brothers,
owned a wife and a cottage of stone where Gaelic was spoken
and turf fires kept everyone warm from the sea's malice while
they waited for fishing tides to bear the curraghs out to the
sharp fins in the skinny dark on the mackerel banks.

A baby's first clothes must come from the distance and a
second hand crib and the village must spit on the child
God bless him. It was luck and the custom and no one
farther from Aran than Marcus in Australia who sent fine
wool and a cradle of coachwood and the special wives
wove him a shawl and a rabbit played on a flute the day
he was born, the rebel song Skibbereen and eyebright
flowered, hoary rockrose, wild madder and seakale. It was
lucky they said as they spat on young Patrick.

The paddocks were full. A great harvest for Ireland, Inishmore, Inishmann where the mainland stopped and westward
the islands of Hy Brazil came and went as Patrick the netmender watched.

"A fine family" they said

"the fairies are kind to old Michael God bless im – his bride
bore nine brothers – and cousin Marcus went to Australia."

Maeve Callaghan cried out "The tubers are blasted with fever.
I do strive to blind them with boiling but unfit to eat they are
with the stench of the blight from Dingle Bay to Garryowen."

and they said on the island "The fairies have come."

A million died – at Ballinrobe, Kilcolgan, Loughrea, Westport,
Longford, north in the Curlew Mountains and all over Ireland
– and many are not equal to one.

Offshore on Inishmore they ate the Connemara pony called Yellowman, the heavenly cow and her calf born on the ice islands with no bull save in Galway and Gort – for strange things happened on Aran even before The Starving. On St. John's night it was by the blackthorn and death answered death through the generations – it was mostly the old and the young.

A million died where once men went naked to fight for the land of the harp and the green flag now land of corncrakes, rack-rents, landlords and winter

where it's only weather for gulls and gannets passing over the churns and cradles by the south wall and the humour of Paddy-with-the-left-leg and a wife's sharp tongue – but in spite of white water on Glasson and rain shawls on the Mull of Kilronan, Michael took the two-oared curragh with two sons for a fishing and no word came back to the brothers and no body floated up for two weeks and never

and they said on the island "the fairies have come and Fergus and Sean will not visit again".

The young brothers fished where the Abbert was only a tinkle and Inishmore far off and salty and the older brothers ran with the tides and "Again the fairies will come" old dark men said who knew of the telling of tales from fathers before them.

The last brothers alive were three fine men, one with a son and the dead don't hurt with the bodies themselves folded for rowers to find and not find.

The last brothers buried the old woman Maeve with her sorrows, stopped the worn clock, said goodbye to beds that were empty of pipers and fiddlers.

Donald   Robert   Patrick

came to Australia and brought Aran with them.

Aran – recalled from hackle back Mount Seaview

Rock islands gallop from the fanned sea
Death horses set over the buried
Stone markers on ash earth

Patrick cried out
as if it were only yesterday
and not 600 AD
St. Enda was buried on my Inishmore

Over his cross a horse carving
lives with the wind
There's another
north by the Church of Four Beauties
and the Seven Churches of Onaught
where my father worshipped

It was yesterday

Come down Cunderang

Two boys, Kevin aged 13, son of Robert
the other Shamus O'Brien
often argued the merits of their two ponies

Callaghan owned a small Connemara pony
Yellow Elf Shot
O'Brien rode a little tatter-mare
Skillywidden

I will indeed admit your mare
is faster than Elf Shot
Kevin would say
but only it is
when the yellow colt's got four on his back
and your brown mare but one

They agreed
only between themselves mind you
to race from Swamp Creek to Mount Seaview
and not be tellin their parents
  the same course
  legendary bushman
  Marc (nicknamed Jack) Callaghan followed
  to meet Merle-Ellen Hogan
  God rest her
  she that died the very minute of his entry

    Come down Cunderang
    by East Fitzroy
    New Connaught
    by the Creek of the Dun Cow
    and Stony Batter
    (brumby sparks by The Wild Spur)
    balanced on saddle and strap
    on a bridle-less ride
    by the Bat Cave
    up Bull Ant Spur
    Terrible Vale and Nuggety Gully
    where Merle-Ellen
    held Jack's hand
    in delicate praise

and to be sure Your Honour
young Callaghan said
twas where the gold colt
lost the brown mare
as if it was Charley Lambert ridin
and not but me own small self

      Then down Beckett's Cataract
      and Joyce's Creek
      "where art be detriment
      to fresh and simple garbs of nature"
      through stands of bastard box
      and ribbony gum
      in all 2500 feet vertical for 6½ mile

and if he got himself lost
and vanished into the earth itself
without leavin so much as a hole
to show where he'd been
to be sure it was his own fault entirely
for puttin himself on a path
where none but a fool would go
though I wish I'd never agreed to the race
knowin as I always did
the golden colt would win
even if it was but me own small self on his back

      Shamus was never found
      nor the small brown tatter-mare
      though it's said to this day
      there's a trace of her
      in the brumby herds on Werriker Mount

and indeed Your Honour young Callaghan said
to the visiting magistrate
an even if I am after tellin you Sir
it's a bloody record we made
me and the gold colt

the darlin little boy that he is

Woollen house

The wind tries to unstitch a wall
my grandmother knitted to keep out the cold
the same wall
my father darned with his life
A hole my toenail made
cut out and repaired

My knees wore thin places
through which he saw the world
filling woollen calendars
        January
        February
        unpicked
        June
        July
        stitched in

Near the wall from my grandmother's time
(her mouth the warmest wool I ever touched)
words came out
                knit one
                pearl one
                plain
                cast off
                reverse the bask for luck

She knitted a roof to keep the chimney warm

I wore that woollen house half my life
rooms friendly to touch
        her labour of wool
        a sculpture made to last

Ripe fruit and a bottler of a pigman
(Mount Werrikimber, 1890)

Martha Callaghan was, to everyone except her husband Robert, a demure matron of praise. To Callaghan she was the big apple – 18 stone dressed or undressed – an orchard of serum and spice – always a January tree ripe after blossom and rain, full of syrup and sap, wet as spindrift, warm as the honeys of Capricorn, applewine addled – a basket, a barrell, a fruit bin, a tree filled with laughter – one shake and Robert was brandied in mellow, claret-skinned, sun-hot applewine.

Callaghan, a wily litle pigman, voice soft as a sow's udder, whispered piglet-children to the broad acres of her belly. Her touch a tango, her beam two-bites-and-a-bit for a pew on Sunday.

He was a bull, a boar, a stallion. One mouthfull and apple-sauce flooded his tongue, a slug in a sluggery that spread silky ink in her foam till his gullet ran silver, tissue-fruit, applewine. She was a fruitshop, a basket, a barrel – and he, the picker and packer, slicer, preserver – a bottler of a pigman, a guzzler, a glutton of pietime in appledarkness for winter nights, islands, mountains and summer.

Cunt-happy Callaghan rocked and seasons rotated. He rocked the big tree the way a great heart rocks in a racehorse when a jockey rides hands and heels on a home run and didn't he just keep doing it.

His life was *Martha,* Rome Beauty, *Martha,* Gravenstein, McIntosh, *Martha* again and again, *Martha, this minute, this second in arms and legs wide as Australia I love ya*

and the hills would breathe out and the house smile with a smile quiet as the puppy-fat dimple on Martha's left elbow.

The song of the woman of the house

Tow row row
Robbie come to breakfast
Robbie come to tea
I need you in the nursery
to rock baby on your knee

Tow, row, row
Robbie will you now
take me this minute
while I'm in humour

Kiss me on the garter
and take me again
There's more lovin in you
than fifty younger men

Take me in the hay shed
on grass thin and fine
buckle me around you
till we're ninety nine

Play me like an Irish harp
but only play the Gauntree
for Robbie when we both be dead
they'll surely play the Goltree

Martha aging

Fill in shadows
with dusk's silver apples
See
bronze sails of wheat
setting out slowly
See
panes of sun
close the road back

Time
reach into me
down my bony fingers
sift tawny ash
over my face
make rivers laugh
day write on the sky

Fill in shadows
with dusk's silver apples

The 9 rivers of Vernon County

Boys catching brown carp
     the only sign
     cork bobbing
     not that they thought
     of the dying
     that diffusion
     vast spill
     all its parts

and who replace the cats
     watching down black eyes

that bony fish
sometime hop back
into it's OK
goodbye cat
in front of the future

St. John's Eve

On St. John's Eve
a woman in white
with a sigh more like the wind than breath
and mournful
beyond all other sounds in the world
leaned on the window sill
and a hoodie crow perched
on the ridge of the roof

and Martha died

Her body lay in the front parlour
quiet as a dingle in Kerry
after the dark men had hunted
the coveys and brakes

Cousins came to watch the priest
sprinkle holy water on warm summers
nailed in the wood
with the big laugh

and children kindly as sorrow
shared the coffin uphill
to the east of the ferns and the foxes

and left Robert alone
tied to his hog days

and a face blurred beyond memory

Robert bereft

After Martha's death the humour went out of his mouth and
his eyes lost their jewels of sperm. Colt-pixies stole cattle.
Horses went wild. Dingos howled near the sties and sometimes a rabbit played on a flute at the grave.

Soon there was only an old man to talk to and that was
himself and didn't he walk straight up the hill many a time as
if nothing had happened.

Martha had left with some of the oldest poetry in the world
still on her tongue God rest her and wouldn't there soon be
time enough to be joinin her with the foxes coming late for the
chickens and he by himself

and what would he see all night but the stars
for maybe a year or two
and by day
the sorrows were cruel to watch
with no one to visit
and the darkness back again soon
and no one to sit with

and he'd say I'll be married again
and wouldn't a wife be as handy as another thing.

The old boar

Apple country above the dawn
high land striated with light
Callaghan spread out his arms like leaves
blown over the woman he loved
kept his pigs in a dimpled sty
and the old boar didn't he
just corkscrew up them in the slops

Callaghan fell down in the mud
he lay there for a day and a year
where his heart gave out pigweed grew
and the old boar
didn't he just keep on doing it

When they found him he was half eaten
they'd eaten the apples out of his eyes
and he was given a grave and a tear

and the old boar

and the old boar

Poem for Martha

Now mandibles of bare fruit trees
just brush new snow
Railway sheds
huddle together for warmth

Martha's shadow whispered a path
by morning elms

On spring nights
she pulled on the sleeve of a plover's cry
then left only a name
in syllables of sleep

An old dress strains to come back
to a room filled with great trees
touching a door
to secrets in the apples
which hibernate near worn out footprints

Bard and storyteller

When the grass was green in spring and brown in summer
the Irish engaged in the sport of hurling
Young Patrick Callaghan was local champion
After an injury he took up the flute and the fiddle
and later was King of the Pipers
(though on occasions disjointed his drones)

He'd put on his pipes and play tunes of the fierce water-horses
from the sea, fairy colts that chased cattle thieves and indeed
he would say, isn't it burned in our memory The Famine, the
glory of the heavenly cow and a horse the colour of honey they
ate to save them from starving and wasn't me father after
tellin me of the magic appletrees of Galway with gold in their
roots – surely the same as those growing in Cunderang

and he said when Marcus imported from Connemara a lady
horse with a golden stride she called to the King of the
Stallions (him with jewels in his semen white as frost on a
fern) the Callaghans laughed and gurt diddicky that old
appletreeman fathered a whole orchard with one seed.

Winter nights Patrick sat in the corner of the great chimney
at Kilronan Station and warmed himself on the richly
coloured skirts of women with cheeks like the rare white
heather found only in the dells of the gentle people and hands
cool as seakale on the dunes of Killeaney. He'd play and he'd
sing, everyone joining chorus after chorus of ancient songs
with the moss still green upon them, while friends did reels,
hop-jigs and slip-jigs, occasional set dances and hornpipes till
the big house rocked with happiness – and laughter in the
long light of the moon would grow old and the notes of the
Soontree fall over the hearth and the red coals sleep in white
ash of spent wood.

He sang of rabbits playing on flutes to soften the pillow,
children changed into swans, ice-borne Connemara rocks,
magic cures for bodily ills, holy wells and crosses on sacred

ground and tractable ponies the colour of flax when they danced with shadowy figures in the leprechaun light of summer stars and of the great Charlie Lambert and wasn't he after tellin he'd win all the races from the Curragh to Cunderang quicker than it takes a silver-white appleblossom to fall in the sun when the old appleman laughs though I'm sorry your honours for drawin your names down he'd say to the children who listened to myths he recounted

though mind you not one of them believed all the words he said though all of them believed every word in the song "Marcus diggin for gold" and that was a favourite he often sang to all alike for in Cunderang English and Irish migrants were woven together like the rough grey and blue garments worn on old Aran

and on special occasions and being the bard and storyteller he was he'd sometimes recite for Charlotte-Maeve Callaghan the Eleventh Century poem from the Book of Lismore written by Cael of the Red Branch to win the beautiful daughter of the King of Kerry though against the advice of Finn Mac Cool

> *The colour of her dun is the colour of lime,*
> *Within it are couches and green rushes,*
> *Within it are silks and blue mantles,*
> *Within it are red gold and silver cups*
> *and ale the colour of warm cherries.*

Running axe whetstone and a spider sulky

Irishtown
        hawthorn
sheep that hungry they ate men

and Duval from the caves of Lascaux
        parted the great sea of Gaul
        came to Irishtown's economy-shaped landscapes
        and said while building
        "Mountains and monuments need the sun"

        Carpenter
        Visions of a city
            under his cooking pot
                mauls
                wedge
                shingle frow
                mallet
                gouging adze
                for a trade in mortising
                running axe
                whetstone
                and a spider sulky
           built as a taught thing
              with legerdemain
              to exercise power

and there his shape and change of face
took in the multiple view

The massacre at Black Hill and the Mountain Rush
Dark Siding called
        Then and there said
        "Out of pity destroy them
        our poor and savage creatures"
        while doing so
        gave them appalling forecasts
        of hunger and frenzy

Then
solemn as a bucket of ice
said "Dreaming demands the ultimate act"
ran a horde over the gulch
at Blowfly Bend
buried rifle shots next to them
in black earth

    So fine and whitely his lambswool beard
    hunted with the pack
    in at the kill
    earned his place at the banquet table
    kept faith with the brutality of men

        Saw this from a turret
        above his eating hall
        as an edifice
        someone else had seen

I know what he looked at
born before his time
Massacres
as in the Guernica painting
grey on black
man holding lamp
revealing mother
with child's body
mania
horse-head
bull
sword
broken teeth
spike-tongue
hand without nail in it

    Jesus on the dialisis
    since time

Marcus Callaghan and the big fish

Duval built on corroboree ground
Right on it
He was a wild dog
took all his land from the Crow Tribe
    with gunpowder
    and a lease
    by the grace of God
    and Queen Victoria
  Greetings
    she said
I grant and demise unto Claude Duval
(subject to reservations)
     and that was the catch
     where Marcus Callaghan
     hooked the big fish
     GOLD
     an eye for profit
      fine women
     to whom he'd say
     and you're very welcome
     and so you are

1872 at Duval's mansion Marcus
kicked a stone under the pepper tree
saw glint in quartz surruptitiously
took out rights from The Empress of India
    to dig sink drive excavate
    GOLD
    pay rent for
     GOLD
    as witnessed by the trusty and well beloved
    Governor Knight Commander
    of most excellent orders
    of St. Mick and St. John (KCMG)
    Commander of Jerusalem and Cunderang
    Signed "X".

Then thick with love for shillings
added pennyweight per ton
Measured profits with tapes a mile long
spoke to balance sheets
in a voice that polished waiters in restaurants
Walked knee-deep in currencies

and punched his body
across the conference tables of Europe
Sent a shaft through Irishtown
dead centre in the eating hall

     Duval died after that
     Mrs. Duval washed the body with tears
     and long acres of useless leasehold
     an old woman walking the winds
     through sheep camps and dingo packs

     * * *

The mine gave out
Marcus surrendered his rights
and gave the mullock heaps
     the bora grounds
to black and equal daughters.

Ghost town – 1945

     For eighty years
     wind has scratched the diggings
     with dry fingers finding nothing
     Under the pepper tree
     a colander of shade
     strains the sun

     Here Eamon built a zoo
     to hold the shock of a fox
     colours of caged birds
     locked in his eyes

     Near a gantry wheel
     drunk Jeremy Wilson
     rinses his brain in the heat
     jailed days in front of him
     repeating by heart the past
     wishing it never happened

     Each year the pepper tree
     creates its own myth
     Summer sings it to sleep
     where the shade of a Callaghan
     dug out the long reef's fire

Footway on Inishmore

Every spring
curious grass
explores cracks in the path
It knows all the weak spots
better than a moneylender

Birds sing little jewelboxes
filled with blue eggs
and a white tree
sails under a full weight of blossom

the day's glove just fits
the fingers of a red apple I hold

Then it's autumn
air cool as a mushroom
Time to leave
just before the weather
turns over in bed

The gospel according to Seaton Callaghan

Take Dingle Bay
as a point of departure
or arrival
    for the land of Beulah
    on a celestial scale
    and Oden as Asgard's hall of the fallen
    House of gold and glad men
    lit by sword's light

    You may fight for a day
    feast on poetry
    to heal wounds in a warrior's back
    and here in Seaton
    (Third Son of a Third Son)
    the consecration
    one dynasty after another serialised
    fierce face set in motion
    by gene pools and a track into Cunderang
    above junk piles –
    clapped-out houses
    shuffled on like trench coats
    through habit and a penchant for order
    in the feel of English gardens

        as Seaton
        undone against the sweep of Eaglehawk
        in plus fours and bowler hat
        one rainy day at Cunderang
        put his umbrella up
        and jackeroos in pommel slickers
        tranced and wincing
        changed him to a beautiful thing

here his useless sword
        2 duelling pistols
        brace bird guns
        snuff box
        crest and seal
        war medals
        prayer book
        poems
        monogrammed writing case
        beret

scarves and suits and walking sticks
hunting horn
whisky flask
pearl tie pin
old letters
                    tied with a blush
                          a garter
                    confessions of love and affection
                              from Beatrice
                              the words
                              yours forever
      and a casket lead-lined
      to return a body home

Once courted Lotty Grace and learnt
      that to kiss a widow
      is a very dangerous thing
      the height she held her skirts
      a traffic hazard
            came to court
            in new and handsome silk
            for the same demonstration

When remittance days passed
sluiced at Nuggety Gully
hydroling and fluming
                  goldfever and grief
                  dragged him into old age

After the suicide
Limerick O'Brien cut down
his bed of saplings
carried him through the Common
with a saddle strap

            Face mutilated
            left side blown off with bird gun
            on the fence nearby
            parts of brain
            hung like grubs
            and Seargent Bean said
            "from an examination of the body
            I concluded him
            to be dead"
nailed up for a lonesome journey

Seaton's reverie (Nuggety Gully)

Life ends and silence begins
Only darkness crosses the gorge
Winds run into cliff faces
Rocks cling to their own shape
Here nothing knows what it is

The blaze of a far river
has no reference point
Art as a taught thing
cannot focus on it
Untouched in the earth
it does not know what it is

Over these hills cities
keep faith with architects
The young and the old hint
at what they will become
memory cold to touch
       cold outbursts of glass

Seasons live in a word
Here there is no voice
no particular hour
nothing to correct the clocks
Here nothing knows what it is

Irish diamonds

Look down a hill
or balance on Cory's Crest
    Sheep drill through landscape
    Old flocks stencil themselves
    on ancient woolpacks
    A caterpillar plague waits for dawn

Year 1900 in Callaghan's store –
    "Pratt's Chart of Chords
    & Giant Album Five Shillings"
    teaches the organ to play
    with Bloater Paste
    Albert Sardines
    Bologna Sausage
    Vencattachillum
    lobster-in-paper
    Bath's Baking Powder
    Borax Soap
    Aberdeen Butter
    Pinkhead matches
    Irish diamonds
    Ell's antpoison-and-hairtonic

Dr. Kitchong sleeps under dateless stars
A snake in a parrot's cage waits for Mrs. Duval

Yesterday gone
like the mayor
stiff with ambition
so too The Demonstration
for Hospitals which care for Good Templars
and Jesus save total abstainers
Those who can't help themselves
go for the shearer's cheques

        The nut-guessing competition
        lies safe in the chemist's
        snug against trusses and jockstraps
        douche cans
        stiffeners
        bandages
        crutches
        and Chamberlain's Cholera Syrup

which makes expectoration easy
and cures
                diarrhoea
                snake bite
                liver cough
                impotence
                menstruation
                debility and the itch

                    alongside the Testimony
                    John Cory shouted as he died
                    with fourteen leeches on his back
                        "I was sinking fast
                        with unpleasant thoughts one
                        symptom
                        trouble ahead another
                        a bitter taste in my mouth
                        and I have not suffered since"

Dr. Kitchong
snores with his reputation
for curing
fits
piles
madness
ruptures
Bright's disease
and veterinary complaints
with a magic capsule and enema
no obstruction could ever withstand

    Joe Bachelor an English remittance man
    hangs from his rafters
        a plaster on his heart
        and under it
        the photo of
        "a lady"

Green jacket reels and a jig

Two full moons will fall on this March
and the Annual Dance
fill woolsheds with flags
          evergreens
          ribbons
          forgetmenots
          blue bows
          songs
          and sweet briars
          and O'Leary
               honey sweating
               and having the knack
               of making even chairs
               conscious
               of their bare legs
               will dance
               with Charlotte-Maeve
and surely there's nothin but limpin
compared with an Irish jig

and Maureen may sing
My name is Poll Doodle, I work with my needle
and if I had money tis apples I'd buy
I'd go down in the garden and stay there till morning
and whistle for Johnny the gooseberry boy

       then form two lines
       and break into reels and long dances
       and slip-jig so lightly
       to "Hare in the Corn"

       tis backwards and forwards
       to jigs and set-dancing
       Maeve and O'Leary
       two fine horses prancing

       Turn right and then left of them
       sideways and circle them
       the fast and the slow of them
       the lick and the go of them

and after a sit-down dinner
eat debutant's cake
and Charlotte-Maeve drive off
in O'Leary's old car
40 HP chain-drive Fiat
with two gears
right in and right out

    and others leave
    in a two cylinder Humber
    or a Flanders
    or a Sunbeam
    or the huge ship of a Renault

        Gold hearts
        motto brooches
        chatelaine bags
        and the smell of Loveskin
        delaines
        Piper's soap
        zephyrs
        cashmeres
        and voiles

The price of experience

Except for cattle-duffing few major crimes occurred at Cunderang. Tofts was hanged at Tamworth for murder. Occasional charges were laid against shearers for drunk and disorderly conduct. There are records of convictions by the travelling magistrate for "Furious Riding in Oxley Street".

Even gold fossickers behaved with a decorum commensurate with their status. Violent deaths resulted from sulky and horse accidents, tree felling, drowning and the like. In none of these instances were criminal proceedings instituted, nor were civil actions for damages taken.

On St. Patrick's Day, after the mass, Charlotte-Maeve took a basket of fairy-cakes to the diggings of Three Legs O'Leary. James Rowan Callaghan compiled an account of the incident from testimony given by old Maud Callaghan and others.

It was a fine day it was when she said goodbye to ride from 'Roran with the new saddle on the golden pony "Kilean" – a present for herself – with one blue eye and one black eye and the gums still as a sentry and all the summer-shadows sharp as a young man's sight and the air clearer than egg-white and her hair yellow as the dappled flanks of her own fine horse and a mischievous smile like one of the green children wavin goodbye Aunty Martha fit to make me heart sing.

From old Patrick Callaghan the rest of that story is said in the idiom he used and on Aran a storyteller speaks always in the first person as if he witnessed every detail.

That O'Leary, him with songs like sonnets in his throat, not a one for marryin, pannin gold in the gully lonely as a wind talkin to the Liffy and the hymn of himself liftin sand for the rockers
and as I was told and Charlotte-Maeve herself said, she rode in and stepped down for the time of day to take tea and a friendly talk

and later the Callaghan boys come up after they heard what she said e done – and with them, stinkin Calley Puddlefoot – him that was charged with sodom on the sheep, a grin with no teeth in it and his cankle cantled like a carved cromlech on Onaught and skin-the-divil-in-me, as big an tight a bull-stick niver ave I seen an e did scream that Legs of O'Leary whin they stripped im bare an spread im on a old triangle used to bull-whip convicts for the doin of what e was good for – an them hoodie crows, cross a Lambin Creek took away, and the wooly sheep as knew what that wankerman was wantin took theyselves to the ridges, and gurt diddicky the little porry cows a snortin at the rest they'd ave from im, spinnin that rape fella, cold an fish thin, an by the Lord e was in im a mile thin some, while they hild im with Cully doin the dance a the bear that grunts

but it wasn't so much what e give im
that Legs O'Leary
as what the fella'd come to by it
with is braggin mouth shoved in the ridge
an is ass fit to bust
with the big thing e was bein taught
it was the thing uv it there an in is touch
face yalla as flat Billy-button weed
an lips gravebone brown

It last, for the first one,
only a tin minute time for Puddlefoot
but for that O'Leary
all the rest uv is life
thin they burdizzoed im
and thin e rest Cully the Puddlefoot
ready for more
an thet was the worst one
blood down is legs all over is belly
and whin they lifted im up tha ooze
wuz drippin outa im

thin the Callaghans got an booted the be jasus outa im
    They didn't quite killim
    left im naked
    bleedin
    but by the lord a the hoodie crows
    that Puddlefoot did giv it to im
    holy an rip up – an they never see im agin

an I'll niver fergit ow them four big
Callaghan boys stripped im off an

one on each arm
one on each leg
lifted im
and tied im to thet rusty triangle
an slam on the hard ridge-rock for Cully Puddlefoot
(an i niver smelt anyone quite as bad as im)
to rip up
an snore on is cry-baby face

an that pretty little voice pleadin
an the green flies
all the time it took
not to be hurt iny more

That is my story

BOOK 2

THE LAND OF THE EVER YOUNG

Says myself to herself "The day is a gold man"
Says herself to myself "Sure you'll never be old man"
Says herself to myself "The world's a white pearl"
Says myself to herself "You're ever young girl"

Zero to infinity

All harmony begins with one note or chord. The order of the rhythm may proceed from zero to infinity in every direction. Patterns may be simple or intricate. Every sense is needed to apprehend the content and the tensions between the parts – but once a great harper strikes one string with his fingernails sounds will reach from the racetracks of the Curragh to the Plains of Pleasure seen on a clear day from the crest of Mount Werrikimber.

Praise the rabbit plague

They were everywhere
under the house
burrows through every fence
    They ate the vegetable garden
    in one night
    AND WE ATE THEM
        snared them
        netted them
        trapped them

        hunted them with dogs and sticks
        burnt them in logs
        mattocked them out of their burrows
        set ferrets on them
        shot them
        belted them over the heads in their squats
        damaged and dismembered them
        flattened them under wheels
        trampled them to death
        wrung their necks
        ran them into corners of fences
        battered
        assaulted
        stoned
        stunned
        decapitated
        and killed them in any way possible

Skinned them
        boned
        scalloped
        stewed
        baked
        roasted
        boiled
        grilled
        baisted
        braised
        devilled and curried
        stewed stuffed garnished
        broiled and spiced them
        salted

                steamed
                casseroled
                            and ATE them

        For a change
                    shinbone marrow on dry bread

                    turnip soup
                    potato pie

                    home made tomato sauce

        and on every cheek
        the hue of a foxglove

The liars of Cunderang

When I was 5 Howdo came and
                    said he'd killed the tiger snake
                    in Mrs. O'Brien's garden
Gran said he's a liar and wouldn't know how
to kill snakes
                He said he'd seen Carlyle Callaghan
                full of blood at the cottage hospital
                    burst with the pressure
                    it went everywhere
I suppose that's why
they won't let children into hospitals

Uncle Danny told me all about himself
He said he could kill a man by touching the death nerve
            designed the Golden Gate Bridge
            went to New Guinea in a U-boat
            as a member of the secret service
            and spied on German armies on the Somme
            even studied geology at New York University
            and taught Howdo rock formations on Cunderang
            Yes – worked on a death ray too
            and could flick a snake's head off
            like you crack a stock whip

I told Gran and she said
                    Daniel's a skite and a liar
                    never been past Mount Seaview

When he heard what she said
                he rolled up his trousers
                    showed her the bad leg
                            and mysterious balm
                            a Zulu witch doctor
                            sent him from Africa

and one day
                he hung his braces
                over an old chair
                and never came back

James explains some intricate facts

On my first day at school
the Headmaster said
>   what
>   does your father do
I said
> chops wood for the fire
> washes the car
> milks our cow
> kills snakes
> and on Sunday afternoon
> watches cricket
> on the town oval
>>   below our house
> and says "shut up"
> when the-lady-next-door
> calls her children
Eenie Eyenie Elvie Edna Merle-Ellen Ray
and
Y-a-l-l-e-r-m-a-n (her little dun cow)
and
Yabba Yabba Mangy Dog
>>   born at the junction
>>   of the Muckeye and Mehi

> and sometimes goes to the races

Once I heard him say
children were more important than anything

> He said this
> and our mother cried

Braids and pickled livers

In 19
the Governor called on Cunderang
representing the King
> who owned all land coloured red
> on the map of the world
> a uniform braided with gold
> and a strange hat

> We lined up at school
> before
> the Union Jack
> and said very fast
> "I honour by god
> I serve by king
> I salute by flag"

> When we did
> his face smiled
> and breathed hard
> on my sister
> so that she cried

> He was very big
> I couldn't do anything

It was a relief
when he left
to visit
Morton's shearing shed
although I don't know why he'd bother
with all those flies

and stinking sheep

> We heard he got drunk
> fell into a thorn bush
> and went back to England
> covered in blood

When I think about it
he must have been quite impressive

Warm scones and a cold feeling

Gran said Charlottle-Maeve Callaghan
   drowned in the washpool
   where they scoured sheep
   before the shearing
   They looked everywhere
   and she floated up
   like a surprise

They buried her behind the deserted house
and wrote 16 on her

When it's quiet
she plays with an eerie sensation

Once I stayed with Gran
at the new homestead
and went down to the old house
shut up with a mob of sheep
in a paddock full of summers
rivers and books by Thackeray

There was a high-pitched whistle in the big room
   no noise
   only silence
The sheep had gone with the sun
I was alone

I ran through summer
  to the new house
  with Gran making scones

It stayed cold long after

I don't believe in ghosts myself

They don't die till sundown

When I was 8
        I killed a big brown snake
        hit it near the front gate
        It got very savage

In summer they get very venemous and bite sticks

     Then old Mavis O'Brien
     came up our hill
     for afternoon tea

     She always walked head down

     My sister curled it up
     on the path
     It was six foot
     Mavis stepped right on it
     and threw her shopping away

          She reported me to the police
          and schoolmaster Michael Stephen
               Callaghan
               gave me the cane

        big fat yellow belly twitching
        right until dark

All the same
they don't often make brown snakes
six foot

Young Donald and a ball of dough

He sits on the riverbank under a willow
String dangles from the pole in his hand
Next to him in a kerosene tin
one silver carp swishes its tail
The cork bobs
He jerks the pole
bait gone
Carefully he takes bread from a trouser pocket
rolls it between thumb and forefinger
places a ball of dough on the hook
drops it gently in the water

Nothing beyond this moment
nothing before it

For hours he sits on an old floodmark
summer in his lap
The day is a reel of slow lace
       dragged from the bend to the bridge
       water moving with the easy gait
       of a grandmother –
       Callaghan's Pool full of sorrow light
He holds his breath
counts to thirty two
A chicken hawk cuts through his thoughts
He forgets the next number
For a long time he looks at the hawk's path
through broken air
He knows August winds are racehorses
       rivers summersault six times
       in December storms
       and when rain stops
       ponds wear white shirts in the moonlight

At night home is a catalogue of old rooms
He sees the flightline of a meteor
       fog spinning webs across the flats
He dreams the river is a silver dish
              polished by stars

His father wakes him

He looks for the first time
              at the Southern Lights
        learns two new words
                  Aurora Australis

Back in bed
he hides the day
in a secret place
no one will visit

Patiently the carp
rinses its life
in his sleep

Meat

I remember the day Robert Callaghan said
to his son and me "You two can butcher
that ol porry in the woolshed
paddock – here's the gun"
handed the .22 Remington to Sean
That was at breakfast time
Then he went off to muster his wethers
along the river flats

It took us half an hour to drive her
into the pen with the gallows
and block and tackle
She knew we intended to rip her right down
That this was the last day
she'd eat ripe grass
buckets of sweet bran
molasses
chaff
lick salt of the earth

Our first shot missed the brain
buried itself in the left lung
She smelt her own death
sharper than kine heat
warm dusk in oats
head down
wild eyes spinning

*   *   *

It is a very long time
since that day at Kilronan Farm
and I have seen meat in supermarkets
in plastic trays
on TV screens
served up with sharp electric knives
sharper cooking smells
and almost forgotten the second shot
that ripped the brain pan
the way she dropped
when all the strings gave in
and what one hell of a job
to winch her up

slip the skin from her back
by twelve noon

covered with blood
how even in late winter
flies came out to watch
as we hacked through ribs
                    diaphragm
                    anus

huge gut spilled out
and kelpie pups rolled
in acid
    urine
    shit

By five o'clock we'd hung the skin
cleaned her up
and the gorged dogs
had vomited muck

Bob rode in and laughed
took the gun from us
wiped it clean
axed through the spine
quartered the beast
and swore by god
he'd do it himself next time

Journey in a salt pot

School vacations
we hunted "The Black Brush"
camped in a bullocky's hut
ceiling hand-lapped oak
walls newspaper
frame ribbony gum
purlins bastard box
table of sassafras
cedar doors
opening on silence

lyre-birds
       mimicked
              band saws
              car engines
              axe-blades
              bull whips
              not guns

We shot and salted them
killed a red fox in the sky
saw brown pine hauled
      up timber trails
      bullock's eyes rolled
      leech
      tick
      leaf
      fungus
      old wood
      wongas
      wild turkey
      no grass inside the scrub
      no sunlight

Nights
      earth warm with laughter
      we sat in the fire-place
      big logs under camp ovens
      looked up the chimney at stars
      watched the bullocky's face

His daughters were love to us
riper than possum fat
mild as rice puddings
Two cattle dogs eyed us
licked dirt floors with their bellies

We slept in chaff bags
dingos howling darkness

    hunted slippery eels
    by planet and zodiac
    sharpened number eight fencing wire
    hooked them with carbide lights
    Salted with adolescence
    shut them tight in a well

We found our way by instinct
through darkness and firelight
broke the moon in half
held onto the south star
pulled horizons around us
rubbed shoulders with sky
backed the wind's racehorse
watched storms one night
killed snakes and a dingo
bragged to the bullocky's wife
took the game home

    Mum cooked it
    for Dad to eat

Now only the foxes' lightning snarls

Flea seed and a hydromel dream

In summer of 19
        the Indian hawker came
        with antiphlogistine
        orris root
        flea seed
        ipecacuanha wine
        spices and Chamberlain's Balm and Tubules
        which make the body laugh
        and cure malignant wasted systems

        and Fortesque & Son demonstrated
        their Automatic Poison Cart & Bosco Fumigator
        which won
        the Grand Champion Field Trials at the Show

          When father saw it
          he was going to be a dogger
          and bought a hundred weight
          of Rangeford's Dingo Decoy
          which everybody used
          to store in sheds

Same year
Vinegar Bob
        with the hydromel dream
        and a wallet
        stuffed with rabbit and dingo money
        went to Sydney
        to meet a secretary
        in clean shoes
        smelling of fine scent
        and bought soap

He stayed at Usher's
where waitresses served him real breakfast
and a choice of everything else he wanted
which cost him the earth

Electric storm on a summer night

On the racetracks
              of my childhood
              flaming horses
              riderless at the night's wells
                          gene-pools
              going back
              further than many lifetimes

Thunder far off
lightning tines
              rippling hackles
              on the razorback

Movement becoming shape
              golden foals
              manes whispering to one another

Stallions
          growing into what will know
                only itself

while a storm-wind visits the lamp
in my red window

History lesson

The horse was crude stone and the windows
of history worn thin by Ramesis III
in a hunting cart with reins waisted
to free his hands for the bow and conquest
        great balls hanging
        like the fruit of centuries
That way chariots were the forerunner

        same way Jack Callaghan
        on Yellowman's back
        after scrubbers
        reins on croup
        flying and balancing
        on Werrikimber Mountain

Also the horse as mark of kings
Saracans Aryans Hittites
Sumerians of Dravidic origin (2800BC)
where stands Kazakstan Onagers and Kish
and Seals on the sovereign papers
        drawing a cart full gallop
    horses as the full display of wealth
        that after Equus Caballus
        the essence of wildness

        Horse pictures at school

Connemara ponies
always flying and balancing
wind in mane
flank close-up
balls tucked in
dangerous occupations

Father

My bleak father used to sit
watching cricketers
spin themselves out
trying to time himself
on an average innings

Our house on the hill
interrupted half the view
where he lived jobless
with a bitter sense of farce
refusing to take the dole

One day
without a word to us
he packed his bags and left
the last sixer
I ever saw him play
better than Bradman at his best

A man of intelligence
he worked factory shifts
making ball bearings
lost the toss
on the process line
slipped on the crease

easily caught off guard
by a savage leg break
that turned grotesque
and gangrenous

Only Aunt Edna
watched him die
once in a while
on rare visits
she could barely afford to pay

Junk tin an' money 1929

We were immobilised by poverty
practically every house
junk tin and money
a poun an rich enough
to buy a month's food
for a big family
backyard chooks and vegetable gardens
next to the dunny
hard rocky soil
water drawn uphill from the river
in kerosene tins
rusty watertanks
full of bungs
rotten iron
fences held up with saplings
old clothes hived through years of handmedowns
patched over patches
blankets like hessian

No one could leave
We were anchored
not even the price of a fare to anyplace-at-all
The sick died
or recovered
in drafty wards at the Cottage Hospital

Old Brasel caught with his pants down
by winter and the flu
Cussie Coyne keeping him warm
for the goldfinch-drenched morning

but the coma had its grip
and stiffened him to meat
in one hour

They couldn't dig a hole to bury him
till after the thaw

The ultimate view from a hill – 1930

On "the one day of the year"
our old car
moved "with a lightsome awe"
      across the scopes of Cunderang
      past the blacks
      on the corner of Oxley Street
      to the church
            with the wheezy old pump organ
            sounding like god
            breathing
            through a very bad lung

      On "the one day of the year"
      Catholics
      Anglicans
      Methos, Callaghans, etc.
      climbed Golgotha Hill
      to remember dead Anzacs
      who used to starve here too
      before they went off
      to be shot
      on the battlefields
      of Ypres Passchendaele
      or the Somme

            and have their names
            chiselled
            into stone and forever
            which is always
            a public holiday

To us ignorance
was a system
which began
and ended
on Golgotha Hill
Men only left Cunderang
to go to war
get killed
or gassed
and cough blood
into every winter
of the rest of life

and on "the one day of the year"
up the monument
some Jewish company
sold by the dozen all over Australia
to look solemn
and drink dole money
at the Last Chance Hotel

Everyone knew
they'd been through hell
and the brothels
in Cairo and Paris
and got VD
which came back
to remind them
in was winter
for the rest of their lives

Names on the monument – 1982

That wind
blowing across town
all the way from Madagascar
reads braille on the monument

small indentations in stone

Callaghan
Hogan
O'Brien

Last week
while armies slept
continents away

it dried khaki uniforms
touched battle-jackets
rubbed skins
of gun carriers
stroked rifle barrels

Not one safety catch woke up

Wallaby soup
(from page 27 Great Aunt Martha's cookbook)

Stir in bone marrow and swedes
      spice and a piquant mood
      zest and sting
      and a racy word
for the savour and flash of dateless days
when trees were ringbarked for tomorrow
and never came down
with harrowing winds on our lives

Taste it now
           with a practised eye
for colour and succulence
        Look at your face
        in the tin town
           the graveyard
           shutting out everything

Lace it with drafts and howls of a Sunday
waiting for God and the Father
      in pews and the silence
      under rafters
           and cobwebs
           dusty as the pump organ's lung
           giving a death rattle
           at the end of Psalm 63
    or Howdo's voice
    turning page after page
    of guilt and godliness
    stitched into black bindings forever
        lessons not learned
        by thick farmers
        and all the tall boys
        in the town

    Yes peck it up with tincture of life
           relish of "g'day Jack"
           in thick noontides of January
    add a touch of embellishment
to rank and simple musks of riverbank
           hillside
           saffron
           ginger

          chili-chili
          garlic salt
          cinnamon
Mull the brew with savour of mace
and what applesauce does to a dumpling or pie
Add fine flavour and delicacy
to that nectar of shinbone
              and the facts of life

Now the day is a wild dog

          wallaby soup
          warm as a cud

Comets bandeau and the 9 rivers of Vernon Country

In 19—my father marvelled at Halley's Comet
piercing the darkest word in his language
   plot a course
      strike the sill of the world

           Everything flying about
           Charlotte-Maeve
           spread over the little churches
           Jemmy Wilson's old trench coat
           flapping its wings
           to owl through eerie dusts
           a wrecked town's graveyard
           shaking bones free
           to steer over the boiling land

and the comet flick'd its tail
spat out fiery lights
off into space
the day I cut my sister's beautiful curls
      and said to our mother
       "little Katy's got a nice high forehead now"

Year after year
silk winds from the sea at Diamond Head
hung magic summers over the great hills
night storms wrenched the sky open
centuries trickled down ranges

My agony mother picked autumn
         apples
         quinces
         marmalade jam
         and took to herself
         a Sunday smile

Winter cracked walls with cold
Sheep drilled through frost
in hard ringbarked country
Gales over Hospital Hill
reminded the dying to die
September polished my sister and I
with long days of shouting and laughter

At bedtime we looked at our world through brass bars
             night fitted caps on the mountains
             farms put on warm bangles
             full moons unravelled the darkness
             stars dangled Christmas-bell chimes
             from the top of Mount Werrikimber
             Icing-cake fires of birthday dreams
             shone innocence on Hungry Hill
             above Coopracurrupa
             and the 9 rivers of Vernon County

Now I have crossed the imagination
to a place hung with old summers
                songs never to be sung again
in walking days of whilom life
squandered by Tom Tiddlers

    My father said goodbye to spendthrift years
                 his Aprils
                 his Augusts

    Storms break like thugs
    over forgotten landscapes
    shaped by barbarous words
    of squatters and rouseabouts
    and my grandmother's straw hat
    crowned with roses and bandeau

                    where white frost
                    slides on like stockings
                    and spiders loop their skeins
                    from appleboughs at dusk

Today I open this book
with the hydromel and jaggery of a puff-pie man
    History rises from his windless flame
    burns itself
    into the silence of a bread-and-water time
                mobs of old sheep
                full of liver fluke
                dust in the lands of never come
                back

Today in Cunderang
even clocks are older than wars

BOOK 3

FOX IN THE PIE

It was Marcus Callaghan said
and to be sure and one day
we'll be another Ireland –
a republic of free men

Goltree, Gauntree and Soontree

The first harp was made from the branch of a red yew tree, bent into the shape of a rib and studded with gold and gemstones. Its Cor is the Cross Tree or harmonic curve and from it comes a sound which, if struck correctly, will turn moonbeams the colour of corn and a blue sky black like a young man's eyebrow. Then the Lamchrann or front pillar holding the strings tight – in it love songs are always alive because they tell of a wooing that is still a-doing. The Com is the belly or sound board.

Each string played by itself is a single note though whole melodies may be stroked and by stopping the fingers at different lengths every note in every musical scale is given.

Small notes tinkle under the deep notes of the bass.

The great harpers played only whole tones and these tones skip over the semi-tones the way a foal's hind feet skip over his own front feet.

There's brogue in the scales played by five Irish fingers when they touch the three great notes of the Goltree, Gauntree and Soontree

and a rhythmic law in every phrase that bounces off the belly.

Soliloquy of a Schoolmaster

I create nothing outside myself
The blackboard stares at me
letters structured in geometric shapes
contained in the dark rectangle of its plane
the white shock of an alphabet

Learning shapes is always difficult
how hands fold over one another
gathering together conscious associations
feeding them into the white shock
It is always difficult to love

The rectangle of black slate
moves only in an unconscious space
Letters spell words – Love is uneasy here
It does not touch or breathe
It could be death that was spelt

Easy to shift between the two
An empty wind might shake air into wings
and that is meaningless
against a cry on the banal slate
and the difficult structure of the word death

It begins here with chalk lines
They contain an impossible purity
shape against other unblemished shape
sheltered in the frame
Silent desperate letters
                              creating me

A shape and dimension of Cunderang

Come down Cunderang
by East Fitzroy
New Connaught
Stringy Bark
Bull Creek
brumby sparks by The Wild Spur
Big Hill shearing down crow-fly miles
to Budd's mare's Creek

The map shows
Gerhardus Mercator's craft and calculus
cemetry divided

for heresy
Catholics
Anglicans – dedicated 16.7.1863
other denominations and Chinese
18.11.1892

land cut linear
named and striated
Location "X" No. 568A
Styx over L

All those pieces or parcels of land in the Colony of New South
Wales County of Vernon Parish of Werriker containing the
past and the future on a scale of one to ten thousand and
bounded on the East by a line bearing North at zero degrees
exactly for 70 mile from the tip of Mount Werrikimber at the
head of the Hastings on the South by the sign of the cross and
a line bearing West from Werriker to The Divide on the West
by a line bearing South along The Divide and on the North by
a line bearing East ninety degrees to infinity be the said
several dimensions a little more or less

All rivers tributaries anabranches
all shingle and alluvium thereon
all beds of lakes
estuaries
lagoons
all lands and parts of islands
these were our skies and stirpes

From 6-23 Sep. 1818 John Oxley
at Cory's Pillow up Moonboy
at the edge of Mullierindi's flo' and rush
down southerly of Surveyor's Creek
to the meridian of Sydney
   where congregated hills
   divide north from south
   to descend
   a gradual dictum
   towards similies of sea

John Harris Esq.
18 horses
2 boats
16 weeks food
Mr Evans
theodolite by Ramsden
Kater's pocket compass
sextant
chromometer
the Hon. Chas. Frazer
and artificial horizon
Oxley himself
and the occasional exaggeration in the journals

1928 was

To that time
plain sailing
every day
bucketfulls of love
plows to goffer the soil
butter off the top
of the butterfactory
in the balance of a thing

"Professor" Kemp from the Federal Woolshearing College
in handsome boundary rider's kit
with Baker's emasculators
and tally counter
among the girls and ginghams

caught Lotty Grace
in the golden varlet of his sight
Same afternoon
ate Alice's
cut-and-come-again cake

Then one Monday night
in late January
under a fox moon
threw a lassoo over Mrs Brumby
and tossed Merle-Ellen O'Brien

Against him the reciprocal weight
of Benjamin Carlyle Callaghan
sharp man and banker
born under the black ink of Zurich
with Inwood's Tables in his right hand
His store at Golconda held in balance
by graphs of boom and counter-boom
Laid alchemist eggs a hundred years back
as most malleable and ductile men do
with atomic numbers

eyes fleck'd
with ruby glass
purple of cassius
as fact and troy
All lands and calculus
held in abstract equilibriums
and the dazzle of Bendigo
and Ballarat

To there ritual
for farmers
seasons of doggers
handmedown children
recycling summers

days unmapped
landscapes
of tin and weatherboard

old houses of Seaton and Trapp
always divided
by mortgage instalments

their gold
in lightning
cracking bull-whips on a mountain's back

They pulled this place over their shoulders
its wages perquisites and profits
with Vinegar Bob rabbiter
scratching holes for traps
in a hydromel dream
jaggery bucks full of spunk
in their brindle earth-house
and does warm as cuds

Joe "Brumby" Callaghan

Then
        as fact
        individual men
        expressed peace with themselves
        and no one else

Joe Brumby
                charged with Furious Riding
                in Oxley Street
                up The Buckle at Steep Gap

                His butterfactory became the damn thing
                of his ruin
                his ruin a divinity
                which came out of his art of love

at 90 lived in a skillion house
with Rangeford's Dingo Decoy
and a lady no one knew
except by the name Black Annis
room 12 x 14 + verandah (12 x 16)
and 1 American axe
        4 cwt rock salt
        8 unsold dingo scalps
        (bounty threepence each)
        180 bullock horns
        camp oven
        delft plate
        sauce pan
        3 leg pot
        billy can
        jorum
        crutch for Annis

an spoilers an Sunday afternoon boys
unhooped his cask
broke his clock
800 yards off 1 bag rock salt

        We found his salt in a cherrytree
        dug a hole in ground hide
        put an ear down to listen in
Cunderang sang *It's nothing to me*

Fox in the pie

Here brindle earth
flowered under ancient plowshares
Orchards tumbled into sunlight
Cherrytrees overflowed with fruit

and Edna O'Brien
                    flavoured hills
                    with her spice
                    hair wild as blackbirds
                    countries in her arms
                    hung the days with summer
                    She was Sunday

Old men tasted her apples
ached from singing against her
then folded themselves through their wives

                    The fox in her pie
                    still bites fiercely

Curlew

Time is a shilling today
and a wind rides in
rolling and willowing
to my front door

and tonight
a curlew will dangle his cry
half way to Aran

I don't attribute a dream to England in 1929

Tom Trapp
red-ragger
born loser of a hundred fights
      said
           "Collins House groups
           English merchant bankers
           take *my* work
           what there is of it
           an the dole
           back to rich men"

He descending from Irish felon stock
no fine Hepplewhite chairs
or high art of great artisans
           Turner and Durer

shillings from marsupial skins
           rabbit
           dingo scalp
           crow

Shot anything that moved
drawing his bead finely
on the flank of a poor thing
at the same time fired
without taking aim precisely
saying "You're suckered"
           That he believed was enough

           He dropped his own life
           at the south end of the old town
           and I laughed
                  for a long time
                  when he died
           and a sea wind came up the pinch
           from Diamond Head
           into Cunderang
                  the golden
                  by the back door

In him
           I tasted a mountain emptying itself
           trailing past the women in his life

remembrance halved
with any job he could get

                    into Rowan
                    he said
tongue slow as a touched slug
                    "Trotsky or someone
                    they knew
                    The Phoenix Society
                    people
                    everyone
                    that bloody poor."

and left to mutter
            "We work for enough to survive
            rough life
            this town gives away nothing
            bush all round
            one road
            an that leads
            to scalping dingos
                crow for bounty
                skinning kangaroos
                moonlighting for possums
                etc"

Later that day rolling down Oxley Street
and singing the rebel song Skibbereen
and doing a slip-jig
(hands in pockets)
drunk
swearing
cursing
arrested to cool down
under the beak
who judged
           "if he can jig
           and swear on oath
           he isn't drunk
           only if he can't put his hands in his pockets"

In the same court Hyek Burnstein cried
when the beak let him stay at Cunderang
after he told how The Black Hundred
killed his wife and child in Poland

Same day
Callaghan's boar
drained himself into a sow's pink ear
and Doran died of whiteleg

Tofts hanged at Tamworth
for cattle-duffing
quivered thirty seconds
after the regulation twenty minutes

his last wish
a drink
of the *magic mineral waters of San Joaquin*
said to cure the liver

so powerful were they
his liver was alive three days after he died
and to bury him they cut it out
and killed it with a stick

as Tom Trapp said
"They never break a bear's bones
till es cooked
west of the Cunderang"

Rat bait

Eamon's brother
put rat bait in the wooden ceiling
blocks hand made
oblong as headstones
That old ceiling breathed in
fifty year's duststorms
Tired from the effort it didn't care
that small footprints twitched across its lung
didn't even cough from the itch
not even a whistle

Listening to them he could not sleep
how they came out to steal some other language
which spoke to them in a rat's tongue
sucked up from cargo cults
that would eat their guts out
drown them in their own blood

All night they rolled those gravestones into their nests
a store of wealth to eat
a capital sum invested for their issue
willed down a genealogy of rats
for executors to hold in trust
for the use of
heirs and assigns forever

Strike this. Blow this.

Eamon Bob Callaghan blacksmith
lives in the small house he bought
when he married Edna O'Brien
had ten kids
and lost count

Every day I watch him
going to work
kids
washing
old car he polishes week-ends
Always nursing babies
to *ding, dong, didilium*

Doesn't even notice
the time of day
Hardly ever drinks
Never been anywhere
except the North Coast
summer thirty-three

I told him one day
of all the places I'd seen
ding, dong, didilium

He just laughed in my face
kept on mending the fence
he'd put up between us

and I hummed under my breath
the old Irish song
Rockin the baby that's none of me own

Poor men always prey on each other

O'Brien's neighbour threatened to shoot his dog
They are both poor men
and cannot mend their ways

Each day he waits in his house
just two eyes at the end of a barrel
He has been reaching for a gun half his life
reading signs of death at target practice

Tonight the milky way is a white opal
the moon a Christmas apple in his hand
three black swans on the glass lake of the sky
Next to them a voice trawls through space
        Howdo singing to himself

Poor men always prey on each other

Patiently he has been dying since birth
      with his rusty gun
      his mortgage
      silence tearing his old clothes

Within town boundaries

The town sits on the ground like a gob of spit
cracked Plume Ethyl sign
chickenyards
general store
debt scratched on dirt
Paint itches the backs of houses
not even fit for poverty

Big transports stop
for breakfast at Eamon's Eatery
where the one roadsign
fingers distance
to the dead-end of the earth

On Killingyard Hill meatworkers
stunned for the rest of their lives
yawn at poleaxed steers
they maul and disembowel

Eamon stops
nods at reality
dreams of horses that never win
His face has the same look
as animals about to be hurt

A shack blows steam through its nose
The wind has lost its hat
The town clock coughs out seven o'clock
Roofs drip liquid bells
long rain dangles fishinglines without hooks
to catch everyone
A stray cat tacks through slush

My father hacked his way through this place
My mother wounded her body with work

Winter
Always colder than the last
closer to bone

Diamond Head (N.S.W.)

Many an elder Callaghan sheepman or horse breeder, worn
out by hard work, retired to Diamond Head. It was also a
favourite holiday resort. On a visit there James wrote the
following poem for his Uncle Donald who lived in a small
cottage on the shoreline.

Great fish hunt under my porch
mowong and trag and mullaway

Each night an old man comes out
and standing next to me casts out
gulls stormwarning his days

Waves swing through marred iron
of wrecked ships
Shells open their fans
in the brushing tides
    He doesn't catch anything
    and that's enough

I watch him there against the wind
agates of his love
    in the seagull's lightning
      the storms hair

Pictures on a mantle piece

On cold days I sit near
my father's portrait
in a room filled with husbands and wives
Old faces distorted
by mould and bad light

Over the fireplace a great uncle
You are like him my parents said
trying to shape a son
into something he was not
a blurred leader
finance minister

Next to him cousin Maurice
dressed as Malvolio
played bit parts
fall-guy for clowns and aldermen
ogres in sermons
Married the cold stare of a prima donna
who tucked him under her corsets
and smuggled him into boudoirs and opera houses
then drank him to soothe her tired voice
and gelded him with huge knees
in the matrimonial bed

and Uncle Rory
rolled out like a carpet for important guests
branded with sideburns and war
and a smile that fitted him
like a straight-jacket
always on the right side
of a law created by fictions
which divided one man from another
by nothing at all

Close-up they are all old
parodies of rulers
They wear what they are
in a fashion always fifty years back
ready to carry out massacres
own up to more than they killed

Every spring a cherrytree
is mirrored in glass which covers my father
For one month he forgets the Depression
landscapes covered with mortgages
dead beasts he tried to protect
from bailiffs and equitable liens

His own mother
thought only diamonds and wedding rings
and chose as a model her queen
kept grandpa on a wheel
turned him over and over
a rooster on a spit
In the end
he spun uselessly over money changers
who got the lot

I remember orphans she visited with sharp eyes
tradesmen honed on her tongue for charging too much
Hearthfire softens her face
almost human as I whisper to her
in reflected light

I remember the one kind day in her life
she took from her purse
and gave me

Turning point

Three boys walk with guns
as far as possible
from dawn to mid-day

All morning they kill
whatever crosses their path
A red fox hides
in the rough idea of a den
The shadow each casts
tied to a weatherboard town
by a gene which defeats them
a framework they cannot escape
to the barbed wire of distance
and they cannot destroy the will
which aims a gun straight

Sheep and cattle country
land skinned to the bone
A river slouching past

Each washes his hands in a storm
which visits at two o'clock
Guns lean on a fence
They eat talk and rest
the river mumbles to sheep
Whatever they shot cools

One of the guns falls
explodes and kills a boy

the river slouches past

Race results and a sad occasion

James O'Brien called Limerick
mourns his child
Angel son
thou hast left us
in the coffin
a pillow of immortelles

        The cortege stopped at the pub
        to read the Melbourne Cup results
        Uncle Don put up
        then on past The Common
        to Cemetry Hill
        ink weed
        wire grass
        and the graves of others
        who died from remedies
        in Muskatt's Illustrated Medical Guide

This side of Winterbourne
forty one dingos killed in a week
where Robert tried to ignite the grass
near his hay-shed
It wouldn't burn
and the following day
the holocaust
started next door
and burnt him out

Oral testimony

I mention the dead and they live
They lie in the shade of a lunatic tree
under disoriented sunshine
beneath the roof of bedlam life
reorder the land's contours
redefine balanced hills
break seals on forgotten lips

Memory is no longer recognised as memory
        solid rock
        my own genesis
        chemistry of flesh
        beasts I eat
        clenched in my fists
        under disoriented sunshine
        where my fathers thundered
        in jailed days
        iron branding history on lies of the past
        distrust of experience
        ideals
            shivering ancient words

        There were no books on the Arans
        History passed on by storytellers
        told of horses
        that outran the fetch of the worst waves
        on storm beaches

I say to all who follow
break these mountains into sunlight
blunt knives on the sun
know the smooth air sings

        and as the men of Cunderang
        above the drowned earth
        hear like the hunted
        distinct and clear the hound

BOOK 4

KILRONAN STUD

Below the homestead
an old river snores in its sleep

In it fish the colour of red silk
rushes like cyphers on Chinese scrolls
and many a fine horse drank there
and many a nimble man and woman sang there

The three brothers

In older times a harper might draw milk from a dry cow and cull from the strings the cry of a baby, the death-cry of a hare, sorrow-winds moving in old lost places or the great laugh of the sun on the backs of those in love.

From the Curragh to Cunderang everyone receptive to that music may listen to the voice of a small creature, be filled with wonder and know how the three feats of the harper, although originally based only on the primitive five-note scale, call forth the Songs of the Shee so they'd dance on the raths in the moonlight or circle the crest of Mount Werrikimber nine times and play with horses the colour of flax in the starlight.

Not everyone will hear any of the music but those who do will know the great bronze laugh of the Gauntree. Nothing is too big and nothing is too small to respond to the Goltree or fall under the spell of the Soontree.

All the melodies of the world begin with one note and in every life there is the crying music, laughing music and the music of sleep and these are called the three brothers.

The harmonies sleeping in the strings answer the seasons of the earth and even though only one person knew a tune and he is dead that tune may nevertheless come out of the strings of its own accord and be heard again.

Edna-Maud and Jack Callaghan

The colour of her dun is the colour of lime
within it cedar and rare books
wine the colour of warm cherries
and songs of the woman of the house

Within it are ledgers and bank statements
brands for black cattle, sheep markers
diaries, tags and tally counters
against the mantle the bronze string of a harp

Their garden is the home of many flowers
silver poppies, bright-eyes and children
Within it the music of shoes
a trellis of vines and warm birds
stocks, sweet william and claret-ash
and a chair where any Callaghan may rest

Kilronan Station, bigger than all Aran, extended though a rich valley. Cattle and sheep herds moved on the slopes. There were haysheds, graneries, paddocks of winter oats, pastures of rye, phalaris and clover. Perhaps an orchard had grown from one appleseed Marcus planted and no finer breed of cattle in Cunderang than the Aberdeen Angus Jack had crossed with the little black porry cows Donald imported from Galway late last century.

Patrick, now called *The Little Fella*, was a favourite at the big house. After his wife died and having no children of his own he often left Hungry Hill Stud, on the rough hard slopes of Werrikimber in the care of his nephew Eamon and would spend long days with Jack and Edna-Maud expounding his theories of genetics or telling of horses that outran the stretch of the wind behind and caught the wind in front of them.

Often he said, the horses of Hungry Hill are indeed the Vanished Tuatha de Danann horses of Connaught fit to be ridden only by sons of kings in helmets of gold and mantles fringed with ermine.

The Connemarra ponies imported by Robert had almost disappeared and instead Patrick had line-bred the blood horses envied by Jack, who dreamed of re-naming his station "Kilronan Stud" and of watching the great mares shunt up his hills in the morning and whirlwind down in the dusk to be fed.

No amount of persuasion would induce *The Little Fella* to sell one brood-mare or provide one service to his stallion – not that he was selfish mind you, though he was a great tale-telling man with a silver voice and no worse than his grandfather.

Horse breeder of Hungry Hill

Old Paddy Callaghan the third bred thoroughbreds
talked pedigrees to wombat holes
listed time-form ratings, classic genes
back to The Barb and St. Simon.
Had a stallion called Pride of Kilronan
with a cast eye that wouldn't get up –
twenty years since he saw a winning post

Dreamt of owning a champion
gullet gun-straight on a rails run
pasterns flat along the final stretch
in front by a mile then some

Built a house to shut out the sky
studied blood lines in rooms cool as walnuts
sunset the colour of foxes
paddocks full of thoroughbreds
he wouldn't sell to anyone whatever the price
shone each mare with the morning star
and when he turned for home
darkness was slipping over his shoulder
cold weather running down his back

Always overstocked
grass eaten by winter
topsoil wiped off like a grin
cat-country ringbarked bare as a belly
in-built staying power
lean prepotency
speed
line-bred
in fillies perfectly conformed
colts with the Callaghan brand on them

The dancing of tails

Paddy Callaghan gripped life hard. His touch had flowers in it. 94 he was. To him visible nature was a bath and a biscuit.

Often he came to Kilronan Station for a man of great age needs the wind and the stars and he watched the clovers and rye grass thicken and the golden elms south of the big house warm themselves in early spring and on Hungry Hill the great mares brimming with pregnancies willowing downhill against the weight of themselves and skylarks climbing through all the scales of a jig or a reel with soft winds ripe in their throats – and the distances – farther, farther than the huge walls of Mount Werrikimber where gums grew and wattle and gallowing oaks and the wonder of happenings blue as the mists of tomorrow and the women with their skirts kind to the old good eye and the left leg with tea, sponge cakes or a biscuit under the elms and sun spilling the thick soup of summer where foals are born and the dancing of tails and bot flies tickling fine new legs and manes gusting and galloping tranced with the first of their days – and him staring past the trumpet vine over the curve of the earth and nearly a hundred years thin with the wearing of Januarys and Augusts and sounds of engines far off in the lucerne and the ploughing where magpies and hoodie crows went out for the eating and all the hyphens of silence between while he sat and the shadows kept still and God bless him his sleep and his waking and mares back in foal coats thickened for frost and the snowflakes and the appletreeman planting his orchard, oaks turning gold and brown grass waving goodbye to white fogs, bare limbs and plovers at night calling half-way to Inishmore and back and the sheep and little black porry cows flowing over the river flats like waves on a beach east of the seven churches of Onaught and the men with their dry-as-a-bone costs coming into the kitchen and steaming while the branch of a wild plum scratched the itchy window and the gentle babies God bless them coming up for their milk exactly at mealtime and sometimes before – and the stars – and the stars when the frost threw shawls of white wool from The Narrows as far as the crest of Werrikimber – and his foals growing up and the mares and the stallions then all over again so he wished never would he lose all the seasons with the passing of one man – and to be sure old Patrick won't go – and won't go on forever and never will light be the same as the smile from the old jawbone he set against all Ireland and the world.

He said to Donald (for no reason called Jack)

In every horse there's a beautiful woman
where a man may die
and next day be alive
in the land of the ever young

and indeed the horses of Ireland are the swiftest in the world as are the fairy colts that chase apple thieves though they would never outrun those of meself to be sure.

Then after a while he'd return to a small wizened house in the last days of living and they'd hear him say to a wife long gone "Mary Grace O'Malley I'll be joinin you soon". He put food in the laundry and under the bed in case she grew hungry and a blanket by the cypress in the front garden so she wouldn't be cold in the frosts and often he said though no one could see her "life's richer for knowin you girl".

Truly and faith tis a revelation to hear an old man reminisce when he speaks of the last Irish harper beating a harp with his fingernails and playing the Gauntree for laughter and after it the Goltree for tears and then the Soontree putting everyone to sleep and he'd sing

On the night of my wake there'll be pipes and tobacco
mold candles in rows like torches watching me
and many a black bottle or two

The devolution of Skillywidden

Making a will should not be difficult
perhaps a premonition of death.
Paddy thought of all the good times
people who showed kindness
Mrs. Rusden who crossed the Oxley in flood
to care for Mary Grace when she was ill
the argument with Jeremy Wilson that went on for 2 years
and ended with Wilson's life
regret that he hadn't made up
It started with a simple statement
that Jeremy drank too much
and no offence meant

The solicitor smiled
buried his hands in a mess of files on his desk
and asked "What are your instructions regarding burial"
a routine question – matter of fact
like asking the time of day
or telling his own wife he'd have 2 eggs for breakfast
and shaking his head when Paddy said
"I think Eamon should get my best mare Skillywidden"
not saying that Eamon was a ne'er-do-well
simply the implication in a look
that changed the intention in the will
so by late afternoon
the whole estate was devised to Jack Callaghan

When the ink was dry Patrick shook hands
noticed the secretary held the door
and smiled at an old man
taking care that his walking stick
secured his weight on the ground
before he stepped to the street
with trees the council planted losing their leaves

and the small shops that shut their doors
were ready to vanish in the darkness

Yallerman

The Little Fella died on the green couch by the north window in the small wizened house where he used to watch Pegasus gallop west in the nightsky and just near the day of his death he called "Yallerman come out of the mools" and as the wake thinned to a trickle a leprechaun foal with the bright eyes of a Patrick was born to the mare Skillywidden to be named in good time and when ready and after the small Connemera pony that was killed in The Starving "Yallerman".

Probate was granted and Jack Callaghan moved the Hungry Hill horses to fine bluegrass pastures on Kilronan, built yards, stables, training track, fenced and set aside 2000 acres of land for the thoroughbreds. Being a good manager and delighted with *The Little Fella's* bequest (though he was missed very sorely all the same mind you) Jack soon became an accomplished Studmaster. He hired a trainer and handler and continued the breeding programme already established.

Often before dawn he watched the great mares waiting to throw downhill wild gales of themselves, grass waves flooding and folding under them when daylight stung them with full power and they thrust themselves against the wind's cry pulling the world into loops and gyres against them

Skillywidden flowing through her own rhythm. the colt Yallerman becoming movement full of messages.

The foal matured and impressed with speed and stamina. Other superbly bred mares like Skibbereen, Perry Dancer, Hinky Punk, foaled trouble free each year and the name Kilronan Stud soon became synonymous with winners on Metropolitan racetracks.

Maeve Callaghan's Pool

Today willow trees
just touch the surface
It is spring
Sky kneels in warm sun

Two boys fish
under the gold birthday of a new bridge
the same boys as those
in the bodies of two old men
who stroll towards town
remembering every ocean
in a drop of rainwater

Fish sleep under a bank
where wind snores
on the river's left arm

Now the old men
lean on the bridge
watching the calendar
swing gently
backwards and forward
backwards and forward

Ceád míle fáilte

Today is a deck of cards
   ace in the sky
   a new shirt
   on the racetrack
   Jack Callaghan
   sun in his heart
   autumn light in the grandstand
   odds
   wide as *Australia*
      I love ya

It's the day of The Golden Mile
   thoroughbreds
   bloodlines
   Jack Callaghan
   tall in a runty way
   but spread quite thin
   to a round and practised eye
   Yallerman
   with all the luck of the Irish
   and to be sure
   and God bless him
   and the track
   hard as the Aran Isles

Rich men juggle fortunes for luck pensioners work
through systems and numbers knobblers swear blind
the hot-shot is done clockers tick with track times plus
one bookies spin prayer wheels red to odds-on urgers
know an outsider will win.

   There are touts and the clappers
   shysters and gyppers
   battlers and hustlers
   fixers and tipsters
   muckers and strappers
   spielers and knobblers
   breeders and breakers
   writers and callers
   apprentices
   mild as milk in the sun
   stewards, clerks, vets, photographers,
   everyone

All the world smiles
at the luck of being alive
    and cross my heart
    and good health
    fortune be with you

    and 100,000 welcomes.

The Golden Mile

(Small voice whispering)

(Racecallers voice)

Hello everybody. This is Johnny Tapp from Sydney racetrack and a fine April day it is for the speed race of the year, The Golden Mile, due to start in 15 minutes. The paddock is full. The Member's enclosure packed with the wealth of business and commerce. My word these beautifully bred thoroughbreds shine in the long autumn light and the silks of women and jockeys dazzle. The course is a beauty, gardens in full bloom. The bends in the track allow every horse to travel his best right through a race. There's the favourite High Step, No. 2 in the all purple, first into the saddling enclosure, backed off the map.

Will 'e leave the March winds behind

Skiffelene's jockey gets up in white and black cap. She's by the great sire Jazz Dancer out of that grand old mare Whuppity Stoorie who was a real Amazon.

Will she outstrip the winds in front

Now they're moving up the course proper. Royal Artillery, Irish Harp, Jack of Hearts in the red, Aran Lady No. 3, Honey Bear and what a pretty filly she is. There's Gooseberry Boy drawn the No. 10 slot, White Girl second favourite with the satchel-swingers.

shagged lookin hoss

Stage Girl in the all pink, she'll give them a shake – Sweet Briar with a heart as big as himself, Knockaderry No. 11 owned by Lady Rath, Eternity looking fit enough to buck off his brands, Applewine – his trainer sure knows how to put a shine on a horse, All I Want, Sunday Morning No. 7, the gelding Skywriter, The Baron in the all gold, Yallerman green jacket and red cap

blatter an blash
run for it catch thought

lightweight Blarney Stone with a postage stamp on his back. He's a chance on recent form and can stay longer than a mother-in-law. What a picture they are. They're at the barrier stalls and moving in nicely. Yallerman's playing up a bit. The starter's getting impatient. Yes the boy on top's having trouble holding him and the Clerk of the Course is helping the handlers get him into the box.

The starter's on his rostrum. They've settled nicely. It looks like a start. The lights are flashing. He presses the button. Gates open and there they go on The Golden Mile.

In every horse there's a beautiful woman

High Step's jumped clean. Yallerman's missed the start by 10 lengths. The leader Skiffelene's slowing a bit, then Stage Girl, All I Want a real speedster, Eternity, Aran Lady, Knockaderry. You could throw a blanket over the field. Royal Artillery, Sunday Morning, Skywriter, All I Want nailed to the fence, then Sweet Briar stretched out, Applewine, Gooseberry Boy, The Baron, Irish Harp and there's many a fine tune been played on him, Jack of Hearts, Blarney Stone and Yallerman a long last.

They're packed tight at the 7. All I Want dropping back a bit, Skiffelene putting on the pace she's a gutsy filly that one, High Step moving into second, then dancing along on the outside Stage Girl, Eternity on the rails, then Skywriter bottled in behind 4 others. They're warming up now. Eternity the old man of the field going nicely, Royal Artillery booming along the outside, Applewine clips the heels of All I Want, Gooseberry Boy stretching out after her and The Baron too, right on her tail, if it was dinner he'd be eating rump steak. Yallerman's moving up.

102

large eyes
made of fire

and Sunday Morning's having a rest. They're a bonny sight coming up to the 5 furlong post. Eternity bounding along just in front of Stage Girl, Royal Artillery putting in a claim, Honey Bear given a lick, Gooseberry Boy, Jack of Hearts bumps The Baron and there's nearly a fall, Blarney Stone, Irish Harp singing along, Sweet Briar, Applewine, Yallerman making up ground.

shod with silver
does e touch the turf

Now High Step takes the lead at the 4 sorting out the men from the boys sure enough. Sky-writer's red sleeves are showing up along the fence. Gooseberry Boy weaving and bobbing about. The Baron still eating rump steak. Stage Girl ridden upside down on the rails. Charlie Lambert's pulled Yallerman to the outside, there's nowhere else to go

Even at a galley-trot
swifter than ghost bulls
on Inisheer

then Sweet Briar running into a brick wall, Applewine, Irish Harp, White Girl kicking the turf to death, Royal Artillery ready to go off, Knockaderry, Aran Lady, Blarney Stone, Honey Bear stuck to the fence, Stage Girl's still got a foot in the till. Knockaderry gets through an opening. Yallerman making up for a bad start, Eternity's stretched out like a rubber band. The pace's a cracker. Wright's bumping the favourite along. He's worried now. Knockaderry jumps into second place. Skiffelene's moving in again, Jack of Hearts got the shakes and The Baron's fallen down a hole – but look at Yallerman go, striding down the outside, red cap and green silks.

jewel in his eye
star on his forehead

You'd think Charlie Lambert was out for a Sunday ride. The crowd's gone quiet. Look at him go.

rider with a whip of platinum

High Step's still in front at the 3. Billy Wright's got a cool pair of hands, then Skiffelene, Knockaderry, Applewine staggering a bit. The pace's a cracker.

Royal Artillery, Skywriter, The Baron scrubbing along, then the all pink of Stage girl, Gooseberry Boy having no luck. Yallerman still coming, Honey Bear bitten off more than she can chew. Wright looks over his shoulder and draws the persuader. Yallerman's exploding. You bottler, He's clear of Knockaderry.

weight displaced by motion
returning to perfect shape
thrust forward again
ribs sprung, full of muscle
articulating bone structure
fulcrum, power and weight coherent

Wright's breaking out in carbuncles. The pace's a sizzler, the rest are standing still. Sunday Morning's completely gone to sleep a long last. Skiffelene's going fiercely, Stage Girl's on fire, High Step's veering out, Wright's throwing in everything. 1 furlong left to go and Yallerman's a hundred mile an hour. Never seen a horse run like this.

conformed at the precise centre of gravity
broad head, narrow face, undulating nose
every force in exact parallel

Last start they used him as a pacemaker, well he's sure making the pace now. Everyone's quiet. We're witnessing one of the great races of the decade. High Step's still in front but only just. Now the crowd's roaring. You can hear them a mile away. Yallerman's in fifth gear. You need ice in your veins to ride like this and that's what Charlie's got.

cool as a salmon's tooth

Yallerman's pulling harder than a Collins Street dentist. You little beauty. What a horse. What a race.

head – cradle of the brain

Now he's 4 lengths in front and still pouring it on. What a race. High Step's gone fishing. The crowd's absolutely wild. He's putting in a paralysing finish.

high withers, deep slope of shoulder
tight back, stretched hip,
straight legs

I can't hear myself think in this noise. It must be a course record, an all time record. What a boilover. At this stage you could bring him home with a piece of cotton.

crest at a gentle inclination forward
ears pricked, head finely coupled to neck

He's past the post and still going. The crowd's gone mad. He's killed the field. Then comes Skiffelene a long way back second, High Step third blown up like a toad, then Royal Artillery, Sweet Briar, Irish Harp, Gooseberry Boy, he couldn't get warm in a pie. Listen to the shouting. This is the greatest mile I've ever seen. Break open the champers folks even if you have lost your shirt. You won't see anything like this again.

outran the fetch of the
worst waves on storm beaches

Charlie Lambert's dropped his glasses. Don't worry Charlie, you can afford a new pair. I said to Jack Callaghan before the race that Yallerman doesn't have any of the characteristics of his sire Pride of Kilronan. Jack said yes, he's got 2 ears, 2 eyes and 4 legs and boy he can sure use them. There's the time now – a race record and they didn't give him a chance in the papers. The rest are done like a dinner. As they say in Cunderang you never break a bear's bones till he's cooked. Well you can start breaking bones right now. He's up there with the all time greats – Tulloch, Star Kingdom, the lot, a real iron horse.

eyes warm as air singing on an Aran hearth

You know there's a magic in big races. You never quite know who's going to win and I nearly called it wrong with the autumn sun in my eyes and I'd swear he had an all green suit coming down the straight and sure Jack Callaghan you've got your pot of gold this time.

Little fella told him there was gold under a ragwort weed and Jack with no spade. So he tied his garter round the weed and went to fetch one. When he got back the little one had a garter round every weed in the field, but Jack's smelt of appletrees so he sniffed it out and found the gold sure enough

Jack Callaghan later said "and sure enough I did hear a rabbit playin a flute as he went past the post and a laugh with the tinkle of silver almost like that of Paddy-with-the-left-leg".

Native cats under the floor

That night the celebrations lasted right until dawn and many a black bottle emptied. There were girls named Maud and Maeve, men called Dennis and Daniel and one with a nickname Yallery Brown and tales told of legendary horses, Queen of Aran, Golden Rath, Maglore, Skillywidden, Kittlerumpit and blood-lines back as far as Tracery and St. Simon.

An old musician, Patrick, great grandnewphew of Patrick The Netmender, was flown from Cunderang. All night he played the pipes and the fiddle, sang

> *I buried me wife and danced on top of her*
>
> *I'm a man meself like Oliver's bull*
>
> *Native cats under the floor*
>
> *Bugga fee Hoosa*

and Jack Callaghan did jigs and reels on tables and doors – all very hard on the shoes.

Jack made a speech lapsing into Gaelic and idioms of other ages and surely the world's a beautiful place entirely and a wife Edna-Maud

> *With a touch like a fairy*
> *Milkin the heavenly cow*
> *To tickle a man*
> *And make him mad*
>
> *Tow, row, row*
> *Jack will you now*
> *Take me now*
> *While I'm in humor*

in a voice like thistles and warm as a wind in December with skylarks callin their children and faith it's surely a revelation to listen – and a man to be thinkin his thoughts in such a place as it is and old Patrick from his heart sang the song wild as the Marseillaise and if from the heart it comes to the heart it penetrates

Good morrow fox. Good morrow sir.
Pray fox what are you aiting.
A fine fat goose I stole from you.
Will you come here and taste it.

and with each verse others joined in till the building rocked like a curragh in a storm

and young James Sean O'Brien sang

Off he goes trippin it, up and down steppin it
herself and himself on the back of a door
and he says "God bless her" and starts to undress her
red-headed Maud from fair Inishmore
and Maeve is a fancy and plain is old Nancy
who drags Patrick the piper onto the floor
and there's muckin and messin and knockin and kissin
the like of what's never been witnessed before
Says Eamon "Begorra I'll settle for Nora"
and she says "You'll not you're a divil for sure"
while Danny and Dennis get on with their Guinness
and by morning they'll all be asleep on the floor

Just before dawn Patrick said so quietly nobody heard and if they did they'd not have believed him, that a banshee wailed on Mount Werrikimber just above Kilronan Stud – and perhaps one did because soon after Yallerman's win Jack's life (according to Eamon) was stolen by small green men from the Land of the Ever Young

and added – it was a fine Irish thing it was for him to be doin that it was

ding, dong, didilium

Mount Werriker quarry

We grow old under the casuarinas
an eyelash falls
one strand of hair changes colour

There are no children left
in either of us
only a light
that was switched on
away back
fifty, sixty years ago
that still burns
and will never be put out
though whole mountains
be moved to cover it

At the quarry
they are ready to blast through rock
with some of that same fire
in both of us

Headstones are the history

Robert Raymond Callaghan
died 27 Oct 1898
59 years

A rabbit has dug its burrow
into
Vinegar Bob's
hydromel dream

A tom-tit's nest
hangs from the angel of God
over the tombstone
of Ben Carlyle
and his wife Taretha
and the broken Headstone of
Helen Duval

great names like Galbraith
Alexander
Anthersan Oswald
Bertha
Dallas-Earl
Rusden
desecrated graves
of Martha and Maeve
are blind to Septembers
of cowslips and everlastings
under glass
and the ripe age
of many a Marcus and
Patrick

Jim
Kathleen
Elizabeth
Rosanna and dates of Hognos
and Bernsteins

Cattle graze to the fence
where a grave with no name
nudges the lusty
and illustrious fathers

Limerick

under a wombat's
        hole
    Dr. Kitchong
    incurable

    Lotty

No bible covers the sackcloth of Howdo
Only flies itch the new section
that shines like a subdivision
                terrazzo
                wild raspberries
                Eamon and Maud
        Died 1883
        1878
        Grandmothers
        Uncles
        Brothers
        and sisters
    Charles Hoppy Callaghan
        aged 74 years
Ageless Joe Brumby
        Tom Trapp

A snake
wire grass
cattle and Tracker Wright
Alice
Erasmus Duval

One tree
        Under it
        Jamieson has bought his
        and his wife Margaret Euphemia
        Jim and Agnes Sempill
                Morton
                Elliot
        and a blackberry bush
    Charlotte Maeve and a delicate

and *Eenie Eyenie Elvie Edna Merle-Ellen Ray*

Jack Callaghan
and sometimes Shamus O'Brien
        little gossamer boy
        dancing a reel
        or a jig or two
        at midnight

   Only Seaton is absent
    from this place
     always

   where no one is
    hungry

   Here lies
  James *Rowan* Callaghan
  in loving memory
under newly turned earth

and no one will call
Eenie Eyenie Elvie Edna Merle-Ellen Ray and
Y-a-l-l-e-r-m-a-n
where *Yabba Yabba mangy dog*
born on the Muckeye
lived his skinny life

There are the twelve books of poetry and twelve horses must be learned by heart and no man may be taken into the Fianna till he knows every word in a breath of wind and how a horse may throw grass at the morning star and not heed the cock's cry and be greater in sinew than song as he gathers himself for the win.

Come down Cunderang

BOOK 3

BOOK 4